GRADE **4** FOUR

POWERTHINK

Cooperative Critical Thinking Activities

Written by Kathy Thoreson and Lisa Daly

Illustrated by Gary Mohrmann

D1406716

Editor: Hanna Otero

Cover Design: Kristin Lock

Graphic Artists: Danielle Dela Cruz and Anthony Strasburger

FS112113 POWERTHINK—Grade Four
All rights reserved-Printed in the U.S.A.
Copyright ©2000 Frank Schaffer Publications
23740 Hawthorne Blvd., Torrance, CA 90505

Table of Contents

INTRODUCTION

"There are one-story intellects, two-story intellects and three-story intellects with skylights. All fact collectors who have no aim beyond their facts are one-story people. Two-story people compare, reason, generalize, using the labor of the fact collectors as their own. Three-story people idealize, imagine, predict – their best illumination comes from above through the skylight."

Oliver Wendell Holmes

As educators, our goal is to assist students to become "third-story thinkers." Both the National Council of Teachers of Mathematics and the National Science Teachers Association recommend including problem solving and decision making as major goals of education.

What is critical thinking? Research indicates that the skill most basic to critical thinking is the ability to listen or read actively while continuously analyzing the information being presented. Sounds pretty basic, doesn't it? This ability requires the learner to be able to engage in an internal dialogue. Effective learners can dialogue internally without skipping steps.

Current recommendations suggest that children can best learn critical thinking skills by working in small groups or pairs. Working in pairs forces students to externalize their thinking – to think aloud, and to identify errors and skipped steps. It also teaches students to recognize and edit unsystematic thinking in themselves and others.

The **POWERTHINK** series of reproducible activity sheets is designed to provide cooperative learning opportunities for either small groups or pairs. There are six levels of challenge in the **POWERTHINK** series, allowing you to introduce critical thinking material at a sequential pace.

POWERTHINK has provided you with activity sheets that pertain to the major content areas of language arts, social studies, mathematics, science, art, and problem solving.

The **POWERTHINK** activity books have been designed to provide practice in:

Evaluating Information
Differentiating Between Fact and Opinion
Looking at Both Sides of an Issue
Solving Problems
Making Decisions
Observation
Synthesis
Searching for Alternative Solutions
Exploring New Ideas
Identifying and Clarifying
Setting Goals
Deductive Reasoning
Pre-planning
Giving and Following Directions
Comparing and Contrasting
Brainstorming
Predicting
Organizing Material

Because the teaching of critical thinking skills can also be a forum for truly individual positive reinforcement, on page 63 you will find a list of powerful verbal reinforcers. Use these to encourage your students as they become **"POWERTHINKERS."**

Happy **POWERTHINKING!**

POWERTHINKING

What is **THINKING?**

Thinking can be many things. To see that this is true, try this:

DON'T THINK! Close your eyes for one minute and do not think of anything at all.

Did it work? Did you find yourself thinking about something? Or thinking about how you weren't supposed to be thinking?

So, where and when do you think? In school, of course. That's obvious. But if you're thinking all the time, there must be other times and places for thinking. You are also thinking when you...

- read a magazine
- decide which television program to watch
- climb a tree
- go for a walk in the country
- write a letter
- play a video game
- go on a vacation with your family
- listen to your grandparents tell about "the old days"
- lie on your back and look at the clouds
- get into an argument

Remember: there are many ways to think. And you're thinking all the time.

Now, what is **POWERTHINKING?**

POWERTHINKING is powerful thinking.

The power of thinking is greater than all other kinds of power combined! Think about the person who discovered that a wheel made it a lot easier to move a big rock. That person's brainpower was stronger than a whole team of big, muscular rock movers. You can use **POWERTHINKING** to solve problems that are too big for any other type of power!

Can you remember a time when you used thinking to solve a problem, make a really tough decision, or get out of a jam? Thinking gives you POWER. Power to turn a bad situation into a good one, to turn a defeat into a victory, and even to make someone with hurt feelings feel better. There is no limit to your thinking power. And, there are lots of ways to make your thinking even more powerful than it already is!

Every page in your **POWERTHINK** book will have a little area called **"LIGHTNING STRIKES."** This is the place for you to write down whatever flashes into your mind as you're doing the activity on the page. Like real lightning strikes, these stray thoughts come and go in a split second. So when you have a lightning strike, write it down quickly, before you forget it. Some of these strikes are going to be pretty wacky. But write them all down anyway. You can always cross out the sillier lightning strikes later, or transfer them to a silly thoughts file. But maybe, just maybe, that nutty idea will lead you to think about a problem in a new way. The lightning stike may not be the answer you want, but it may lead you to the answer you are looking for. So remember: write down whatever is on your mind. Try it! You'll be amazed at the powerful stuff that flashes around in your brain.

Each activity in your **POWERTHINK** book also includes a **"POWER PLAY."** POWER PLAYS are questions that will challenge you and take you and your powerful thinking machine one step further.

POWERTHINKING asks you to look at your mind as a muscle. The more you use it, the stronger it gets. If you keep using it, keep stretching it, before long, you'll be thinking with real power. That's what **POWERTHINKING** is all about: learning to use and strengthen your mind. You will find that you can use **POWERTHINKING** at school, but you will also use it at home, during vacations, and for the rest of your life!

FS112113 POWERTHINK

Frank Schaffer Publications

THINK ABOUT THINKING

What is thinking?

    How do you think?

        Why do you think?

            When do you think?

                What do you think about?

                    Where is the best place to think?

                        What are the qualities of a good thinker?

                        Do you need silence to think?

Work with a partner to list as many things as you can about thinking. Write down words and phrases that come to mind. Don't worry about using complete sentences.

Draw a picture of your ideal thinking place.

Write down a problem you'd like to think about.

_____

Describe how you think when you…

a. play chess.

b. solve a math problem.

c. write a letter.

d. build a treehouse.

e. watch a baseball game.

f. read the newspaper.

g. listen to music.

_____

_____

_____

_____

_____

POWER PLAY

When you don't have anything important to think about, think about thinking - on the bus, walking to school, as you fall asleep at night.

LIGHTNING STRIKES

Name(s)_____

ONE THING LEADS TO ANOTHER

One way to use your thinking skills is to look at relationships among different objects. A tadpole grows up to be a frog. A smile may be the first step in making a new friend.

Work with a partner or small group to complete these sentences.

First a caterpillar, then a _____

First a seed, then a _____

First a tickle, then a _____

First a cub, then a _____

Think of other objects or actions that have this type of relationship and write them below.

First a _____, then a _____.

First a _____, then a _____.

First a _____, then a _____.

First a _____, then a _____.

First a _____, then a _____.

POWER PLAY

How can actions be related? If you get angry with a friend, what might happen? If someone doesn't invite you to a party, how would you feel? List some actions and possible results of those actions.

Draw one of your ideas for first a _____, then a _____.

FS112113 POWERTHINK   Frank Schaffer Publications

MORE OR LESS

Some items seem very different at first until you look at how they are related. To **compare** means to look for ways items may be alike.

A crumb is like a cookie only there's <u>less</u> of it.

A hill is like a mountain only there's <u>less</u> of it.

A bud is like a flower only there's <u>less</u> of it.

Work with a partner and fill in the sentences below.

A sandbox is like a _____ only there's <u>less</u> of it.

A bathtub is like a _____ only there's <u>less</u> of it.

Now work together to think of more items that are similar, but different.

A _____ is like a _____ only there's <u>less</u> of it.

A _____ is like a _____ only there's <u>less</u> of it.

A _____ is like a _____ only there's <u>less</u> of it.

A _____ is like a _____ only there's <u>less</u> of it.

A _____ is like a _____ only there's <u>less</u> of it.

POWER PLAY

What other ways are the above items alike? Select one set and list ten ways they are similar.

Look around your classroom or your home. What can you think of that is like something else, only larger?

HOW R U 2DAY?

Many letters and numbers sound like words or parts of words. What letter sounds like a part of your face? One answer could be the letter I.

What letter would you use for a small, buzzing insect?

What two letters could you use for something not difficult?

What letter can you drink?

Work with a partner to make a list of letters or numbers that sound like words. You can combine two or more to make one word. Write the words they stand for.

Letters	Words
B4	Before
_____	_____
_____	_____
_____	_____
_____	_____
_____	_____
_____	_____
_____	_____
_____	_____
_____	_____
_____	_____
_____	_____
_____	_____
_____	_____
_____	_____

POWER PLAY

Did this help you think about words and numbers in a new way? Name some products that use letters or numbers as part of the product name. Why do you think the numbers or letters are used?

Write sentences using as many of your "new" words as you can.

I'D LIKE TO BE A...

Would you like to be an astronaut and travel to other planets? What about a circus clown, a rodeo rider, a bus driver, or a zoo keeper? There are so many interesting and exciting jobs waiting for you.

What kind of job would you like when you get older? Work with a partner. List a job you would like to do someday.

Your job: _____

Your partner's job: _____

Work together. Talk about why you would like that job. What kinds of training would be needed? What types of tools would be used in that job? Write your ideas below.

	Your Job	**Your Partner's Job**
Reasons:		
Training:		
Tools used:		

POWER PLAY

Talk to someone who has the kind of job you'd like. Get some books from the library. Find out as much as you can about the job. What hobbies could you start now that would help you later in that job?

WHAT COULD IT BE?

Close your eyes. Open a catalog to any page. Point to an item on the page. Open your eyes.

What object did you point to? _____

How many different uses for it can you and your partner think of?
List them below.

POWER PLAY

Inventors look at familiar objects in new ways to see how else they could be used. This is a good way of getting ideas.

Ask some friends or family members to think of other uses to add to your list.

Draw your objects being used in new ways.

Let your partner select an item without looking. What was the object?

_____

List as many different uses for this object as you can.

IF I MET AN ORANGE WHALE

Have you ever asked yourself the question "What if?" A **POWERTHINKER** asks questions and looks for new answers.

Work with a partner or small group. Select one of the starters below. Have one member of the group finish the sentence. Then take turns writing sentences to complete a story. Write your completed story on another sheet of paper.

If I met an orange whale…

If I woke up with green spots all over…

If I came to school today and found my teacher walking upside down on the ceiling…

If I were President of the United States of America…

If I could paint my house any color, it would be…

If my shoes walked off without me one day…

If my shadow could talk, it would say…

If I could travel anywhere in the world, I would go to…

POWER PLAY

Did the story end the way you thought it would when you started? Ask one member of the group to read the story to the class. As you listen to other stories, think about how you might have written them.

There are many, many answers to the question "What if?" Write some what-if questions of your own. How many answers can you list for each one?

HOW WOULD YOU CHANGE IT?

Some days, nothing goes right. Did you ever wish you could change the world — or at least one little part of it?

What would you make frozen so it would last longer?

How about a smile?

Work with a partner or small group to think of ideas for how you might make some changes.

What would you…

   …make larger to make it nicer?

   …make louder to make it more pleasant?

   …make brighter to make it more clear?

   …give wings to make it prettier?

   …make invisible to make it go away?

   …put in a rocket and zoom into space?

   …make sweeter to make it taste better?

   …make smaller to fit in your pocket?

POWER PLAY

You can't change the world, but you can change some small parts of it. List some things you can change. How could you change them to make them better?

FS112113 POWERTHINK

Frank Schaffer Publications

WORDS FOR NOISES

Words like SWOOSH, PLOP, and BANG all describe sounds.

However, there are many more sounds that need words to describe them.

What sound does a pen cap make as you pull it off a pen?
Create a word to describe that sound.

_____

What sound does a chair or desk make when you slide it across the floor?
Create a word to describe that sound.

_____

Make your own words for noises with a partner. Write as many words for noises as you can!

_____
_____
_____
_____
_____
_____
_____
_____
_____
_____
_____
_____
_____
_____
_____
_____
_____

POWER PLAY
Create a class dictionary of your new words that describe sounds.

LIGHTNING STRIKES

PICTURE THIS

Did you realize that some words can look like their meanings when they are written in a certain way?

example:

Isn't that cool?

Think of other words that can be written to look like their meanings. Use the space below to draw your words. Good Luck!

POWER PLAY

In small groups, combine your ideas to make a rebus story which includes your favorite picture words. Perform your story for another group. Read the picture words with tons of expression!

Name(s)_____

FILM CLIP

Choose a film category, such as Comedy, Horror, Drama, or Action. Make your friends the stars! Create a cartoon film clip of your friends' adventure.

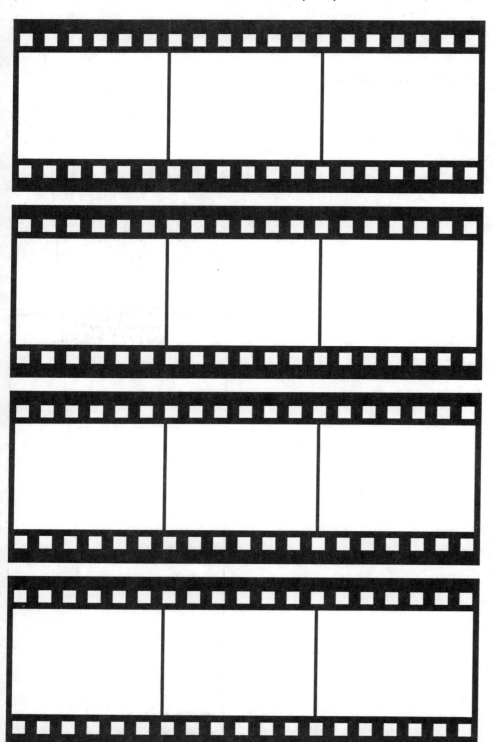

POWER PLAY

Now, using your family or friends as characters, write a "Funniest Home Video."

ANIMAL MIX UP

Can you imagine what an Ape-a-roo or a Kittapotamus would look like?
Think of an imaginary animal that is made by combining two real animals.
Use the following steps to help present your "mixed-up" animal.

1. Create this animal in your mind.
2. Draw the picture.
3. Write a verse or a few sentences about this imaginary animal
   you created.
4. Write the name of your new animal as a title.

POWER PLAY
Now create a new life form using the "parts" on the following page.

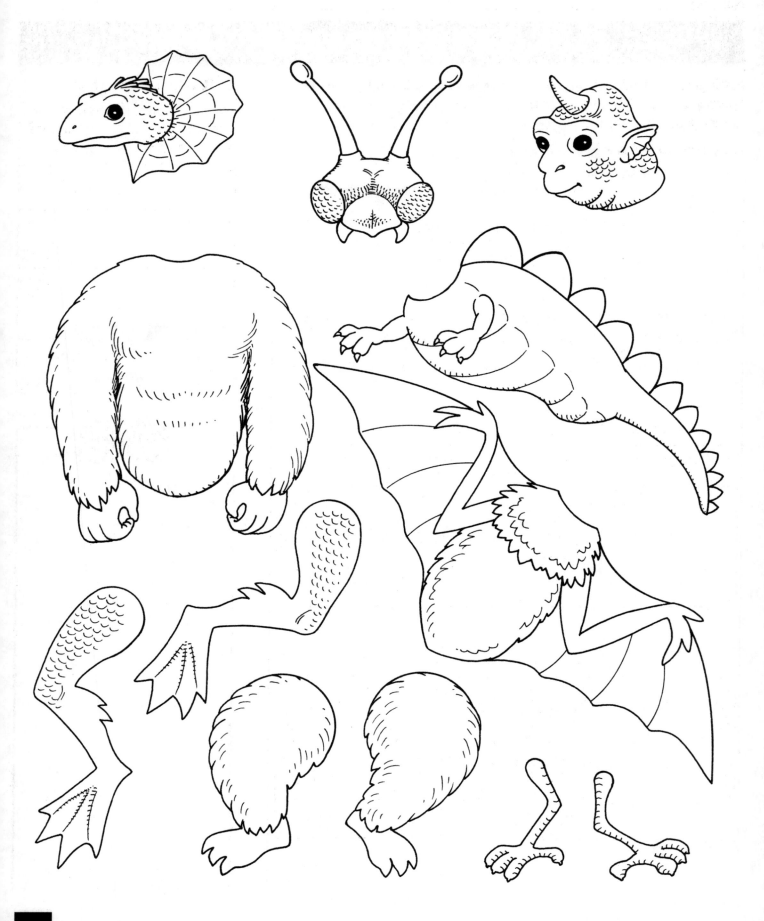

COOKIN' WITH ANALOGIES

Analogies are sentences that have two word pairs. Each pair of words is related in the same way. Analogies are important because they help you to recognize similarities between things.

Look carefully at this example.

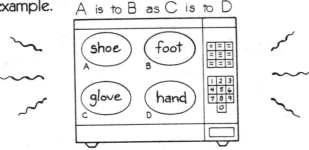

A is to B as C is to D

From this analogy, we can recognize this relationship: A shoe protects a foot the same way a glove protects a hand.

Now! Get cookin' in your groups and start stirring up your own analogies!

POWER PLAY

The analogy blocks below are completely empty. Use your wildest imagination and come up with some original analogies.

A is to B as C is to D

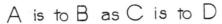
A is to B as C is to D
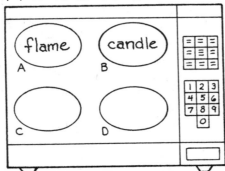

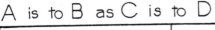
A is to B as C is to D
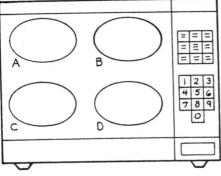

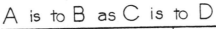
A is to B as C is to D
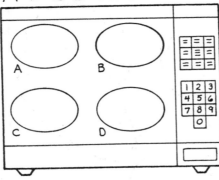

CRAZY CONVERSATIONS

If a prune met a raisin, what might they say to one another? What might a table say to a chair? With a partner, choose two objects. Create crazy conversations between these two objects and write what they say below!

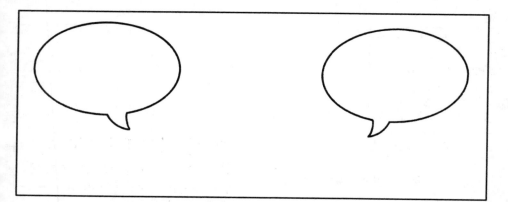

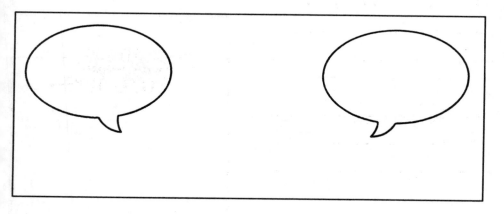

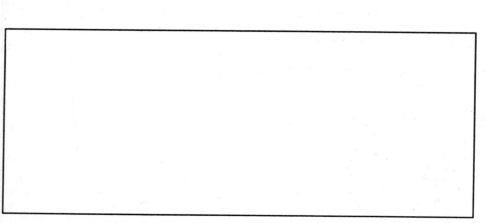

POWER PLAY
Create a comic strip illustrating your favorite crazy conversation.

NURSERY RHYME FOR NOW

Do you remember the nursery rhymes that were told to you when you were younger? Well, now that you are older, and a little bit bolder, let's give these rhymes a few new lines.

Example:
Jack and Jill went up the hill
To fetch a pail of tea.
Jack fell down and broke his crown
And "Ouch!", he sprained his knee.

Hickory, dickory, dock

_____

_____

_____

_____

_____

_____

Rain, rain, go away,

_____

_____

_____

_____

_____

_____

There was a little girl,

Who had a little curl,

_____

_____

_____

_____

_____

_____

_____

_____

POWER PLAY

Choose any nursery rhyme. Begin it in the usual way, but make the rest a little bit different. Illustrate your version of the nursery rhyme. Act it out with a partner or a small group.

"KOOKY" COMPOUNDS

Sometimes compound words are more than just two words joining together to form one new word.

Have you ever seen a "butterfly"…

…or a "boardwalk"?

Illustrate the "kooky" compounds below.

monkey wrench	stopwatch

POWER PLAY

In a small group, brainstorm more kooky compounds. Try drawing them. Time flies when you're having fun!

headline	lighthouse

dogfish	Walkman

LITERATURE LOVE LETTERS

Think of your favorite poem, song, or story. Using the basic letter writing steps, write a love letter to the author! Your letter should include why you love this writer's work and how the work makes you feel.

POWER PLAY

Did you ever read a book that was so good you didn't want it to be over? Do you wish the author would have written a sequel to that book? Write down two suggestions for story lines for a sequel to your favorite book.

COMPARE AND CONTRAST

Compare and contrast various types of literature using a Venn diagram. A Venn diagram can be used to compare or contrast two characters, two versions of a story, or two books by the same author. Below is a list of stories and authors for your reference.

Story	Author
The Strange Story of the Frog Who Became a Prince	Elinor Lander Horwitz
The Frog Prince	The Brothers Grimm
Red Riding Hood	James Marshall
Lon Po Po	Ed Young
Duffy and the Devil	Harve and Margot Zemach
Rumpelstiltskin	The Brothers Grimm
Journey Cake, Ho!	Ruth Sawyer
The Gingerbread Man	Author Unknown Illustration by Ed Arno or Elfrieda
The Three Little Pigs	Author Unknown Illustration by Paul Galdone or Pene Du Bois
The True Story of the Three Little Pigs	Jon Scieszka
The Egyptian Cinderella	Shirley Climo
Prince Cinders	Babette Cole
Briar Rose	The Brothers Grimm
Sleeping Beauty	Charles Perrault
Sleeping Ugly	Jane Yolen
Stone Soup	Ann McGovern
Stone Soup	Marcia Brown
The Mitten	Alvin Tresselt
The Mitten	Jan Brett

POWER PLAY

Compare and contrast two pieces of literature from one of the following suggested authors:

E.B. White	Robert McCloskey
Patricia MacLachlan	Miska Miles
Patricia R. Giff	Aliki
Aesop	Mitsumasa Anno
Dale Gibbons	Steven Kellog
Laura Ingalls Wilder	Beverly Cleary
Shel Silverstein	Wiliam Mayne
A. A. Milne	Dr. Seuss
Peggy Mann	Eleanor Cameron
Anna Sewell	Mercer Mayer
William Steig	Eric Carle
Ursula Nordstrom	Peggy Parish

LIGHTNING STRIKES

Venn Diagram

One way to show how two things are alike and how they are different is to use a Venn diagram. Similarities between the two items are written in the section where the two circles meet. Differences are written in the top and bottom sections where the circles do not intersect.

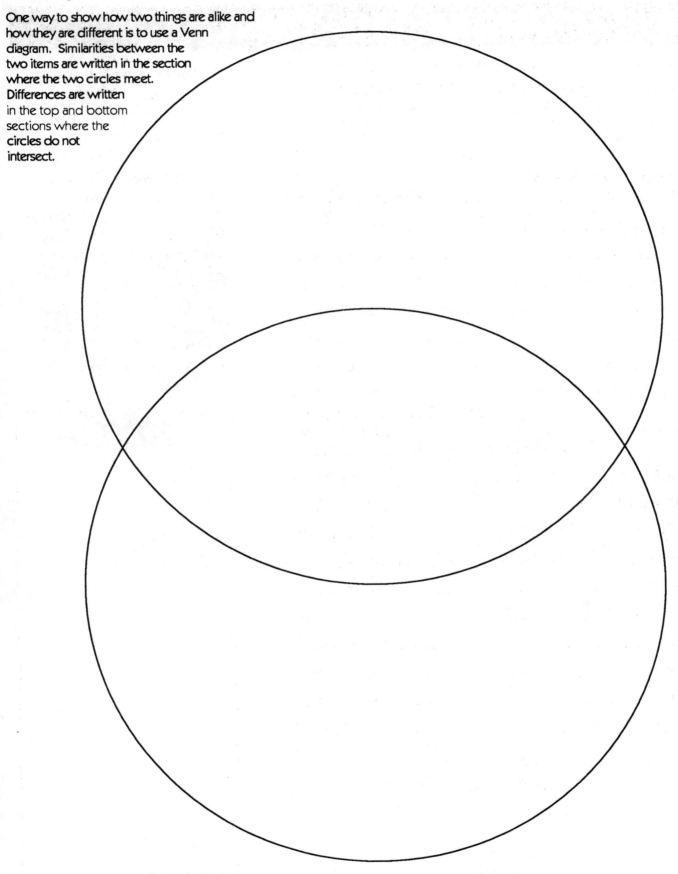

FAIRY TALE TWIST

Fairy tales are stories about magic and wonder, good versus evil, and far-away places. Let's retell these stories and give them the fourth-grade twist.

Jack and the Beanstalk

Give this fairy tale a new ending!

1. Pretend that Jack is running with the magic harp toward the beanstalk. Suddenly, the beanstalk disappears! What is Jack going to do? Will the giant catch him?

2. Discuss with a group what you think is going to happen. Write your ideas for a new ending to this fairy tale.

Cinderella

Make Cinderella a modern day character!

1. Discuss with your group what her family would be like. How will they treat Cinderella?

2. Will Cinderella want to impress someone by getting a new dress? Where will she be going that she needs a new dress? How will she get there?

POWER PLAY

Your group is working for a local newspaper. Write a newspaper article that explains the events of Jack and the Beanstalk. Include an exciting headline.

Act out your story with your group.

IT'S SHOWTIME AMERICA!

Write a commercial to advertise the United States of America. Highlight the positive points about our great country and what might attract people to America. Decide what props will be needed to present your commercial. Use the space below to write your commercial for America.

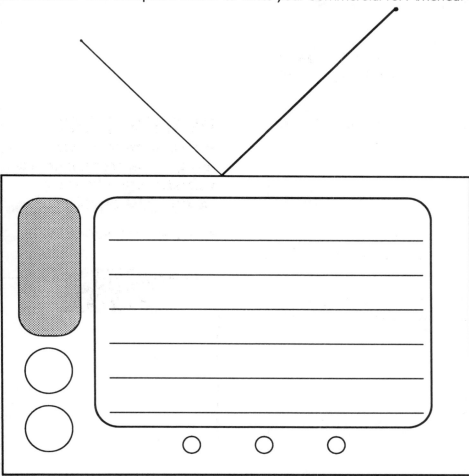

POWER PLAY

Change the words to a favorite tune and make up a jingle for your commercial.

THE GREATEST PLACE TO ESCAPE

Travel brochures are used to highlight the special features of spectacular places throughout the entire world! The exciting information in these pamphlets helps people to decide where they would like to go.

With your group, imagine an original vacation land. Create a travel brochure that describes this incredible place. Include a map with a key or legend that highlights all the things that make this place so special. Mention all of the unique attractions, popular land and water forms, and interesting sites for people to visit.

Use the space below as a work area to record ideas for this great escape brochure. Happy vacationing!

POWER PLAY

Place your imaginary land within the real world. Use an atlas for deciding which longitude and latitude lines will help others to locate your land.

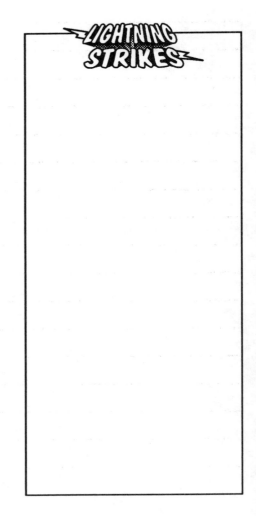

NOBEL PEACE PRIZE

Think of problems or conflicts that have occurred with peoples in the past. Today's problems continue to happen because of social issues, or conflicts about religious freedom or individual rights.

Watch a television news report, read a newspaper or magazine, or talk with an adult to better understand one conflict of today. Make a "Peace Plan" that might solve this modern-day conflict. Explain your plan below.

Peace Plan

_____
_____
_____
_____
_____
_____
_____
_____
_____
_____
_____
_____
_____
_____
_____
_____
_____
_____
_____
_____
_____
_____

POWER PLAY

Create your own symbol for peace! Design a bumper sticker with a slogan to promote peace in the world today.

2020 SCHOOL VISION

Imagine your school in the year 2020. Picture the changes that will occur in the future. What lunch foods will be served? What type of transportation will be used? What will the classrooms be like?

Discuss with your group the changes that may occur. Will these changes affect learning in the future? Why?

Use the space below to design a part of your school in the year 2020. Label its futuristic features.

POWER PLAY
Make a schedule! Include the events of a typical day in your 2020 school.

RELOCATE YOUR STATE

Imagine that your state was magically moved to a new location in the United States of America. Think of a part of the United States that is very different from where you live now.

List the traits of your home state. Now list the traits of the state in its new location. Compare the traits of both locations. Share your answers with a partner.

Trait	Your Home State	Relocation
Food and shelter		
Environment		
Plant and animal life		
Transportation		
Seasons of the year		
Recreation		
Holidays and customs		
Other notes		

POWER PLAY

Coordinate a day of fun to celebrate the day of your state's relocation.

SCHOOL DAYS

Alice was a new student in Mrs. Carole's fourth grade class. Her books need to be stacked from smallest to largest for them to fit properly into her desk. Discuss with your group how Alice can stack her books with the smallest book on the top and the largest book on the bottom.

1. The reading book is larger than the social studies book.

2. The math book is larger than the language book.

3. The science book is larger than the social studies book, but smaller than the reading book.

4. The reading book is smaller than the language book.

POWER PLAY

Describe the sizes of books in your desk. Challenge a friend to arrange these books in size order.

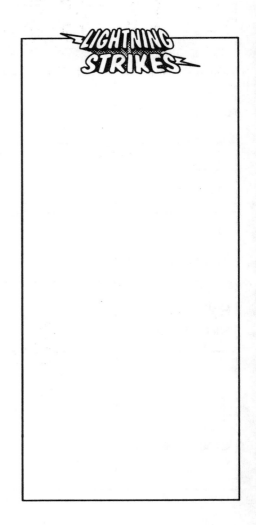

GO WITH THE FLOW

Flow charts are used by computer programmers to map out the sequence of computer functions from beginning to end. Drawings are used to show the sequence of steps a computer needs to follow in order to complete a particular function. The flow chart below takes you through the steps required to blow up a balloon.

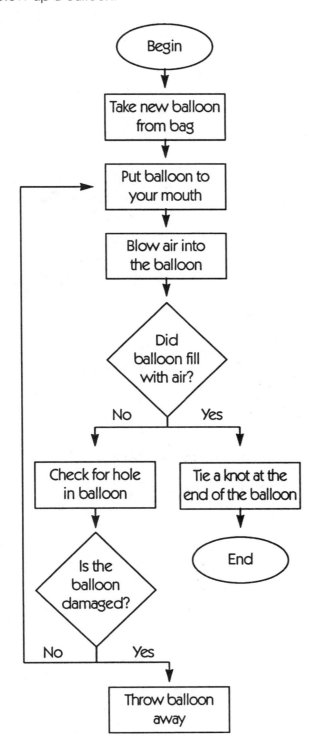

POWER PLAY

When using your balloon which steps did you follow? Why?

Color the steps you followed.

GO WITH THE FLOW

Complete the flow chart below to map out the sequence of steps you would take to sharpen a pencil. Use the scrambled steps to complete the chart.

End

Insert pencil

Take test

Turn handle

Begin

Did the pencil sharpen?

Clean sharpener

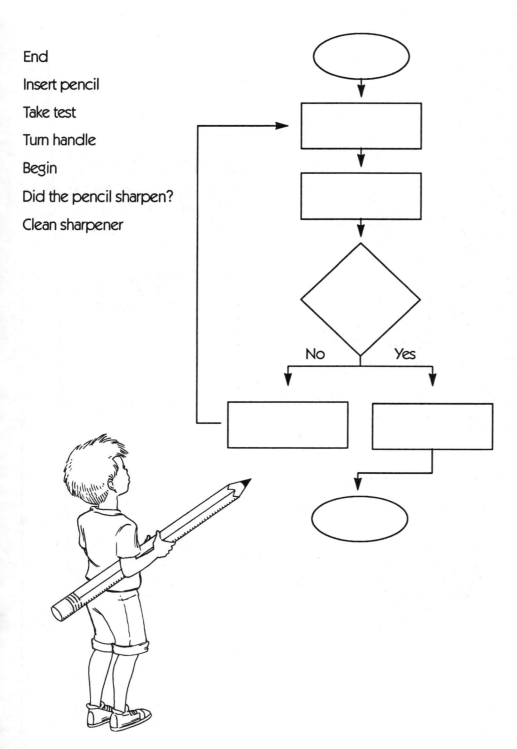

POWER PLAY

On a separate piece of paper create your own flow chart using these symbols:

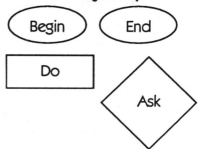

Begin   End

Do   Ask

Think of an activity you do every day and map it out on a flow chart. Remember to go with the flow!

LIGHTNING STRIKES

GOING APE

When we use our common sense, it helps us to understand number sense!

At times a number can seem very big.
(Example: There are 5 apes in your bedroom.)

At times that same number can seem very small.
(Example: There are 5 bananas in the jungle.)

POWER PLAY

In what situation would 1 foot seem like a long, long distance? In what situation would it seem like a very short distance?

Try these number sense challenges...

A. You have $100 In your pocket (here 100 seems BIG).

When can 100 appear small? _____

B. There are 25 books in the library (here 25 seems small).

Where can 25 seem BIG?_____

With your partner, decide how these numbers can be BIG and small.

50

small_____

BIG _____

500

small_____

BIG _____

5000

small_____

BIG _____

FS112113 POWERTHINK   Frank Schaffer Publications

WHAT'S THE SCOOP?

Look at the picture and carefully read each statement. Finish the table by filling in the blanks. Write "True" if you think it explains part of the picture. Write "False" if you think it doesn't explain part of the picture.

	It is chocolate	It is vanilla	It has 1 scoop	It doesn't have 1 scoop	It does not have sprinkles	It has sprinkles
	False	True	True	False	False	True
			False			
						True
	True					
				False		
		False				
	False	True	False	True	False	True
	True	False	True	False	True	False

POWER PLAY

Draw the ice cream cone that doesn't fit the rule. If there are 2 scoops of ice cream then it can't be your favorite flavor, and it can't have sprinkles.

LIGHTNING STRIKES

BUILDING BETTER BODIES

Healthy bodies need to eat from each different food group. Fourth graders need to eat about 2500 calories each day to supply their bodies with energy.

Goal

To plan one day of healthy meals and snacks. Use the chart to include the correct amount of servings per day.

Procedure

1. Collect labels and empty boxes from a variety of foods you eat.

2. Use the Nutrition Chart below to help classify product labels by their nutritional group.

3. Use product labels to count calories while creating your nutritional menu.

4. Decide with a partner how you will display your menu. (Example: You can use a graph, draw a picture, make a list or chart.)

Nutrition Chart
Servings per Day

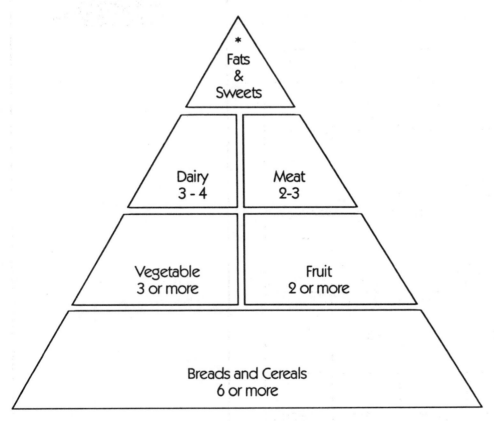

*These snacks are high in calories, but most of the calories can come from more nutritious foods. Eat these sparingly!

POWER PLAY

Share your outcome with the class. Include your opinion.

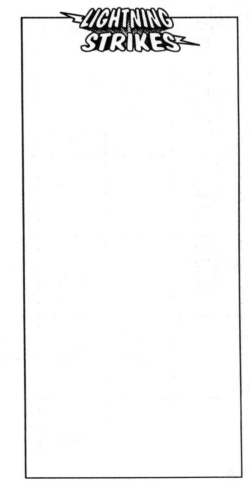

FISHY BUSINESS

Timmy, Shafika, and Scott collected different types of fish at the aquarium. They each kept their fish in a 45 oz. (1.3 kg) water bag. The spotted fish each weigh 15 oz. (.4 kg). Discover how much the striped fish weigh. How much do plain fish weigh?

POWER PLAY

List or draw the fish in order, from the one that weighs the least to the one that weighs the most.

1. What is the total content weight of Timmy's bag?

_____

2. What is the total content weight of Shafika's bag?

_____

3. How much do the striped fish weigh?

_____

4. How much do the plain fish weigh?

_____

5. Why is it important to know the weight of the water in determining the weight of the fish?

_____

_____

_____

LIGHTNING STRIKES

YOU CAN DO IT!

You were asked to stack 45 cans for a recycling display in your classroom. The cans must be stacked to look like a triangle. Follow these steps using playing cards to help plan the correct way to stack the cans.

1. Count 45 cards from the deck.
2. Set up all 45 cards.
3. The example below will help you start your triangle display.

POWER PLAY

Work in a group or with a partner to decide how many cans would be in the last row of a stack of 300 cans. Explain how you found your answer.

1. How many cards are in the bottom row of your stack of cards? _____

2. How does knowing this information help you to properly stack your cans for the display?

   _____

   _____

3. What pattern do you notice from one row to the next?

   _____

   _____

Note: Playing cards are needed for this activity.

GRID LOCK

The surface a figure covers is its **area**. You can measure the area of a figure by counting square units.

Example: One panel of a quilt is equal to 1 square unit. You would need to know the area of your bed to determine how many square units would be needed to make a quilt large enough to cover your bed.

Use the grid below to help solve some of these Grid Lock questions.

1. What is the area of the grid below?_____

2. Cut the grid into its square centimeter (cm²) units.

3. Cut 1 cm² unit in half. Don't discard it.

    a. Will this change the cm² unit shape?_____

    b. Will this change the cm² unit area? _____

4. Use your imagination to rearrange all cm² units into one closed shape.

    What is the area of this figure? _____

5. How many different figures can you make with these units?

    What is the area of each of these figures? _____

6. After making these figures, what important fact can you conclude about area?

    _____

    _____

POWER PLAY

Estimate how many cm² the outline of your hand would be. Then, trace your hand (keep your fingers together) on the cm² paper on the next page and count. See which classmate has the largest and smallest hand per cm².

Have Fun!

Centimeter Graph Paper

FS112113 POWERTHINK

Frank Schaffer Publications

GOIN' TO THE FAIR

Your school is having its annual spring fair. Use the information in the tent to help you solve the problems below.

Cotton Candy 60¢
Pretzel 25¢
Popcorn 85¢
Lemonade large 95¢ small 75¢
Hot Dog $1.25
Sauerkraut 25¢

1. Sam has $3.00 to spend. Give two combinations of different foods he could purchase.

   _____   _____

   _____   _____

   _____   _____

   Total $ spent _____   Total $ spent_____

   $ left over _____ $ left over_____

2. Jimmy and Kristen have $5.00 to spend between both of them. They each want a hot dog. Kristen wants sauerkraut on her hotdog. Jimmy wants a large lemonade. Kristen doesn't want a drink. How much did they spend?

   _____

   Do they have any money left over to buy some snacks?_____

   List the snacks they can buy. _____

   _____

3. For every $2.00 spent at the fair a $.50 donation goes to the school.

   a. How much money has to be spent for the school to earn $500.00?

      _____

   b. Which stand do you think would collect the most donations?

      Why? _____

      _____

POWER PLAY

If you had a stand at the school fair, what would you have to do to earn $100 for your school? Discuss this with a partner.

HABITAT FACT

Could there be an ape in your backyard?

Imagine that the place where you live is at the center of a circle that is 40 feet (12 cm) wide. List all the creatures that might have their habitats within this circle. Compare your list with a partner and discover the creatures making their "Home Sweet Home" in your neighborhood.

POWER PLAY

Choose one of the creatures from your list. Explain how the arrangement of food, water, shelter, and space is important to the survival of this creature.

_____ _____
_____ _____
_____ _____
_____ _____
_____ _____
_____ _____
_____ _____
_____ _____
_____ _____

FS112113 POWERTHINK   Frank Schaffer Publications

ENVIRONMENTAL "WANT AD"

Predict a future environmental problem. What are the current natural or human behaviors that are causing this problem? Create a "Want Ad" to find those responsible. Be specific when stating information on your "Want Ad."

Who?   Who or what may be causing the problem?
What?   What is the problem?
Where?   Where is the problem occurring?
When?   When will this problem occur?
Why?   Why is this a problem?

POWER PLAY
What suitable reward could be given to the person who finds a solution to the environmental problem?

EUREKA!

You and a friend have discovered an exciting new animal on an incredible journey through the rainforest. What does this animal look like? What do you both decide to name it? Why?

Draw your newly-discovered creature below.

Home of the _____

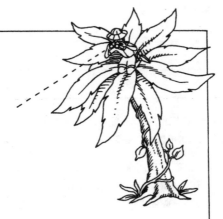

POWER PLAY
Construct a model of your rainforest animal using any materials available.

DINO DETECTIVE

Dinosaurs roamed the earth over 65 million years ago! Today, dinosaur detectives (paleontologists) continue to learn about these incredible creatures by discovering and studying their fossils.

Imagine you are a dinosaur detective who just uncovered a new dinosaur fossil! This fossil shows a huge jaw and sharp teeth. What do these clues tell you about the eating habits and characteristics of that dinosaur? Can you describe this dinosaur's prehistoric home?

_____

_____

_____

Research different dinosaurs. Find out where the sounds of their roars were heard and the marks of their huge footprints could be seen.

Examine the map below. Choose areas where dinosaur fossils might be found. Mark these areas with an **X**. Name the dinosaurs that left these fossils. Explain why you made these choices. What research information helped you to make these choices?

POWER PLAY
*What object of **today** do you think will be a fossil that might be discovered by detectives of the future?*

For a DINOmite time, read <u>If I Had a Brontosaurus</u> in Shel Silverstein's <u>Where the Sidewalk Ends.</u>

Name(s)_____

U-P-O UNIDENTIFIED PLANETARY OBJECT

Hey, Space Cadets! Soar through this planetary chart. Observe the relationship between a planet's distance from the sun and its surface features. Notice that the planets' surface features resemble that of their closest neighbors in orbit.

Planet Name	Distance from the Sun	Surface Features
Mercury	57,900,000 km	dry, dusty, rocky
Venus	108,200,000 km	thick clouds, very hot
Earth	149,600,000 km	water and rocky land
Mars	277,900,000 km	cold, dry, volcanoes, canyons
Jupiter	778,300,000 km	sea of gases, tremendous storms
Saturn	1,427,000,000 km	swirling gases, violent winds
Uranus	2,870,000,000 km	dark, windy, slushy, icy
Neptune	4,497,000,000 km	layers of ice, gases
Pluto	5,900,000,000 km	frozen colorless gas

Use the following page to complete the activity below.

POWER PLAY

Now that you have made up a planet of your own, write a story describing what life is like on this planet. Does the sun shine a lot longer on your planet than on Earth? Or is there a sun? What about the night sky? Do you see lots of stars?

You have created a planet! Let your imagination run wild.

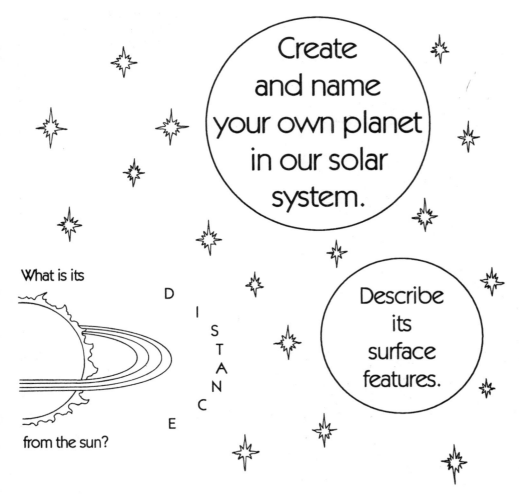

Create and name your own planet in our solar system.

What is its

D I S T A N C E

from the sun?

Describe its surface features.

LIGHTNING STRIKES

FS112113 POWERTHINK   Frank Schaffer Publications

Name(s)_____

PLANET X

Attention all Space Cadets! Before creating your planet, remember its relationship to the sun will affect your planet's surface features.

May your U-P-O turn out A-O-K!

POWER PLAY

Make a model of your new planet. Include a list of items Space Cadets would need to survive there.

IMPROVING INVENTIONS

To invent means to make something new using your imagination. Since the year 1992, there have been almost 100,000 patents issued for inventions. Thanks to "master mind" Alexander Graham Bell, we are all able to communicate with our families and friends on the telephone. Become a "master mind" and make an improvement to an invention of your choice or improve one of the following inventions.

How could you...
- make a telephone better?
- make a sailboat faster?
- make a playground more exciting?
- make a movie more realistic?
- make a book come to life?
- make a bicycle fly?
- make exercise easier?

Discuss your ideas with a partner or group. Illustrate and label the parts of the newly-improved invention using the space below.

POWER PLAY

Invent a machine for something you don't like to do. How does this invention help you? Maybe your invention could be issued patent number 100,001!

Frank Schaffer Publications

Name(s)

WHAT'S NEW IN THE ZOO?

Have you ever looked closely at a kangaroo? Doesn't it look like somebody took parts of other animals and put them together? A kangaroo looks something like a sheep and something like a deer. Its ears look like they belong to a rabbit. And to top it all off, a kangaroo has a pocket.

If you could design an animal, what would it be like? Would it have bird wings and goat feet? Would it have a striped tail, lots of fur, or an elephant trunk? Would it have fins and wheels?

Work with a partner to create your own animal on another sheet of paper. You could draw it or cut out parts of pictures from a magazine and paste them together. You could add strips of colored paper, yarn, or string.

When you finish your animal, fill in the blanks below.

I'd call my animal a _____

because _____

_____

_____

This animal is different because it _____

_____

_____

_____

POWER PLAY

Make up a short story or poem using your animal as the main character.

List some reasons why it would or would not make a good pet.

Display your drawing in the imagination zoo on your class bulletin board.

JUNK IT!

A banana peel, a broken wheel, a three-legged chair, a shoe without its pair, an old car door, and much, much more.

Guess where you are, it's not very hard.
You're in the middle of an old junkyard!

Imagine there is a junkyard that only fourth graders can use. Decide with your group what would be in your junkyard and draw the items below. Don't leave your junk just lying around in that yard! Sort it all! Everything has its place.

POWER PLAY

Collect 5 pieces of "junk" and place them in a paper bag. Switch your bag with another group's bag. Construct a treasure from their collection of junk.

Name(s)_____

SHAPE SHIFTERS

Imagine you are able to change yourself into ANYTHING you wish to be. Picture yourself as a tree, a tiny bumblebee, a new silver key, or anything you see!

What kind of shape would *you* like to "shift" into?

Draw yourself as this shape in your new environment. Present your "new" shape to the class. Explain why you chose to shift into that shape. What are the advantages of being that shape?

POWER PLAY

Shift your shape through pantomime. Allow time for your group to guess your "new" shape.

IMAGINE THAT

What can these bubbles be?

Add to each bubble to make different objects. Draw your object straight, sideways, or upside down. The possibilities are endless!

POWER PLAY

Imagine a bubble that could last forever! What would you put inside that bubble so that it too could last forever?

FS112113 POWERTHINK

Frank Schaffer Publications

A DESIGN ALL MINE

Create your very own design! Here's how:

1. Trace circles, squares, triangles, ovals, and rectangles on black construction paper. Cut them out.

2. Arrange the black shapes onto a piece of white construction paper and glue them down.

3. To complete your design, add string, yarn or glitter.

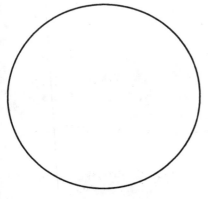

POWER PLAY
To make the design a bit more puzzling, replace patterned shapes with a handful of old jigsaw puzzle pieces.

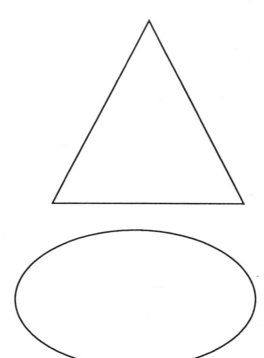

HEY! WHAT'S YOUR PROBLEM?

Everybody has problems! Have you ever forgotten to study for a difficult test? Perhaps a friend hurt your feelings! Maybe you forgot to feed the fish! Oops! These are some problems many people face each day. The more practice you have in solving problems, the better prepared you will be to face such challenges. Go for it!

When you are faced with a difficult problem, what do you do? Take charge! Spark up your thinking skills and make decisions that will help find an electrifying solution.

Boost your brain power by solving this problem:

Chris just got a new haircut. The haircut looks absolutely horrible! Chris and Pat are best friends. Chris asks Pat for an opinion. What should Pat answer?

With a partner, use the following steps to help you to…

Rely on Mind Power to Decide Clearly!

Rely on	**R**estate the problem.
Mind	**M**ake it real.
Power to	**P**redict outcomes.
Decide	**D**ecide what is best for you.
Clearly!	**C**heck your decision.

Step 1: Restate the problem.

To do this, ask yourself: What's the problem?

The problem is: _____

Step 2: Make it real.

Decide what *you* would do if you were actually faced with this problem.
To do this, ask yourself: What would I do if this was *my* problem?

Below, list choices that could be made to solve this problem. Don't limit yourself. Give anything a try!

If my best friend just got a really bad haircut, I would…

1. _____

2. _____

3. _____

4. _____

5. _____

HEY! WHAT'S YOUR PROBLEM?

Awesome job! You have restated the problem and listed what you would do if this was *your* problem. You're ready to move on and predict what will happen.

Step 3: Predict outcomes.

Make an "if…then" statement for each choice listed in Step 2. To do this, ask yourself: If I do this, then what will happen?

Choice 1 _____

If I _____

then _____

Choice 2 _____

If I _____

then _____

Choice 3 _____

If I _____

then _____

Choice 4 _____

If I _____

then _____

Choice 5 _____

If I _____

then _____

Decide whether your choices will cause something positive or negative to happen.

- If your choice has a positive outcome, circle it.
- If your choice has a negative outcome, cross it out.

HEY! WHAT'S YOUR PROBLEM?

Good for you! You've restated the problem, made it real, and determined the outcomes to be positive or negative. A solution is in sight!

Step 4: Decide what is best for you.

Decide which circled choice in Step 3 is the best solution to your problem. To do this, ask yourself: Which choice works best?

- If your choice seems as if it will work, circle it again.
- If your choice does not seem to work, cross it out.

Step 5: Check your decision.

If you have only one circled choice remaining, then you have found the best solution for your problem. If more than one circled choice remains, list all the positive (+) and negative (-) points for each choice.

POWER PLAY
Always Rely on Mind Power to Decide Clearly…and you'll do just fine!

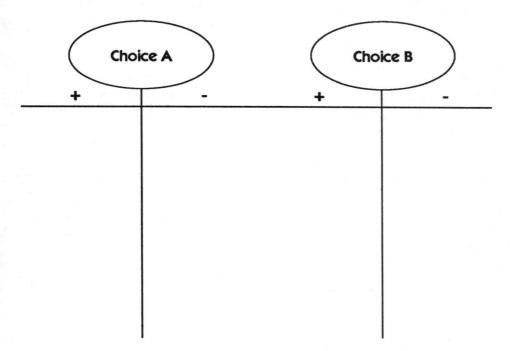

The choice that has the most positive points is the best solution to your problem!

Hey! You did it! Let's review the problem solving steps.

1. **R**estate the problem.
2. **M**ake it real.
3. **P**redict outcomes.
4. **D**ecide what is best for you.
5. **C**heck your decision.

DEAR FOURTH GRADER

Here are some problems that need a solution. **R**ely on **M**ind **P**ower to **D**ecide **C**learly and help solve one of these problems. Thanks for lending a helping hand!

Dear Fourth Grader,

- While Jessica was taking a test, her friend Jeanine asked her for one of the answers.

- Lynn saw an older schoolmate writing on the bathroom wall. The older girl warned Lynn not to tell.

- Robert's brother Jim got an expensive new jacket for his birthday. He told Robert not to touch it. Robert wore it anyway and lost his brother's jacket.

- Eileen had to move in the middle of the school year. Eileen is shy and can't seem to make any friends at her new school.

1. **Restate the problem:** What's the problem?

   _____

2. **Make it real:** What would I do if this was *my* problem?

   1. _____

   2. _____

   3. _____

   4. _____

   5. _____

3. **Predict outcomes:** If I do this, then what will happen?
   Make an "If…then" statement for each choice above.
   - Circle positive outcomes.
   - Cross out negative outcomes.

4. **Decide what is best for you:** Which idea works best?
   - If your choice seems as if it will work, circle it again.
   - If your choice doesn't seem to work, cross it out.

5. **Check your decision:** If more than one circled choice remains, list all the positive and negative points for each choice.

State your solution to the problem:_____

_____

_____

_____

POWER PLAY

When you have a problem to solve, what do you usually do? Think of a problem you had recently. How did you solve that problem? How might you solve the same problem now?

Name(s)_____

THE ROAD TO COOPERATIVE LEARNING

Avoid bumps on the road to cooperative learning. Ensure a safe journey when working together by watching for the following signs.

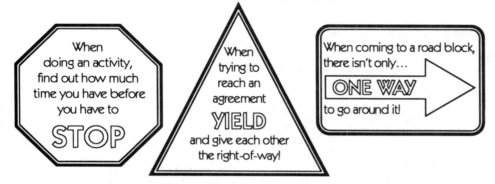

When doing an activity, find out how much time you have before you have to **STOP**

When trying to reach an agreement **YIELD** and give each other the right-of-way!

When coming to a road block, there isn't only... **ONE WAY** to go around it!

With your group, create your own exciting signs to watch for on your cooperative learning journey.

POWER PLAY
Anytime you are travelling together be sure to use your licenses for learning so that everyone knows his or her responsibility.

LIGHTNING STRIKES

NOT JUST SIGHT-SEEING

As you travel on the road to cooperative learning you should see wonderful sights such as: group members sharing, eye-contact, and one person speaking at a time.

What other sights should be seen when on this journey? Finish the scenery that should be along this road. Create a caption for each scene.

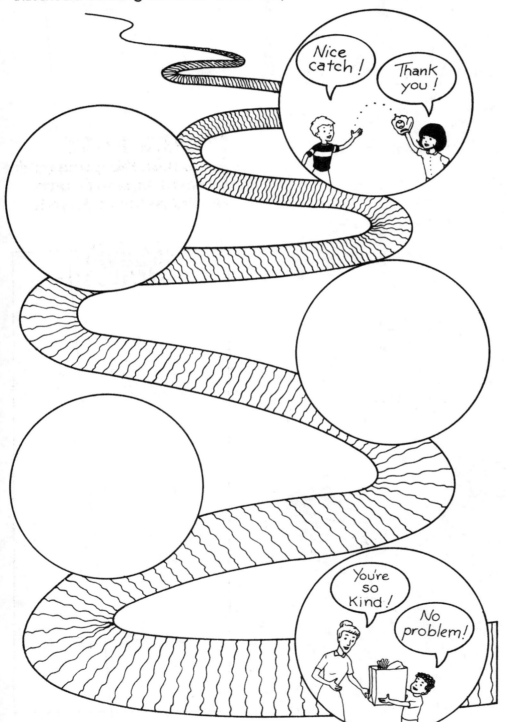

POWER PLAY

Brainstorm ideas that encourage positive thinking. Then design a poster to remind the class to always think positive when working in a group.

MAKE A JOYFUL NOISE!

While traveling on the road to cooperative learning, you should hear sounds of group members...speaking words of encouragement, disagreeing in a kind way, and calling each other by their first names.

If such things were heard on every journey, traffic jams would sound like this...

POWER PLAY
Silence is golden! Make up silence symbols that you can use whenever the noise in your group goes beyond a "joyful noise."

What are some of the sounds that should be heard if your group finds itself in a jam?

Frank Schaffer Publications

ENCOURAGING POWERTHINKING

One of the additional benefits of teaching critical thinking and problem solving in your classroom is that it is an excellent forum for positive reinforcement. Try some of these on for size!

That's an excellent question.

Perhaps that idea would work. Let's try it.

That's a creative way of looking at it.

Not many people would have come up with such an unusual idea.

Terrific idea!

Very interesting thought! Maybe it would work.

I never thought of it that way. Good idea!

That could be just the ticket!

That suggestion makes a lot of sense.

That idea is pretty fantastic.

What a wonderful thought!

That suggestion is quite unique.

That shows you're really thinking.

Let's consider Joe's idea.

Very imaginative!

Splendid!

What a marvelous plan!

Let's consider Sue's recommendation.

Very creative!

Let's give Kim a round of applause for that suggestion.

Very inventive!

Let's follow Tim's line of thinking and see where it goes.

Now why didn't I think of that? Good job.

How did you ever think of such a good idea?

Congratulations on coming up with that solution.

You're very observant!

Your good ideas are popping like popcorn.

That could be just the answer we need.

All right!

That idea shows you're really thinking.

You're quite a **POWERTHINKER.**

Your question shows you put a lot of thought into the problem.

You're really thinking today!

Good going!

That's a pretty awesome idea!

Brilliant idea!

You're very creative.

Great plan!

I knew you could figure out an answer for yourself.

You handled that tough problem very well.

Wow! I'm impressed.

You made a wise decision.

You handled that problem well.

Brilliant!

Jill has the hang of it now.

What an interesting proposal!

This class is full of good ideas today.

See what you can accomplish!

Working together really works.

Well done!

I can't believe all the great ideas you've had today.

Nice job!

Keep up the good work.

That is so outrageous it's contagious!

BIBLIOGRAPHY

For Teachers:

Bagley, Michael T., and Hess, Karin K. 200 Ways of Using Mental Imagery in the Classroom.
   Unionville, NY: Trillium Press, 1984.
Bransford, John, and Stein, Barry S. The Ideal Problem Solver: A Guide for Improving Thinking, Learning, and
   Creativity. New York: W.H. Freeman, 1984.
Mitchell, William, with Conn, Charles Paul. The Power of Positive Students.
   New York: William Morrow and Co., 1985.
Shaefer, Charles E. Developing Creativity in Children.
   Buffalo, NY: DOK Publishers, Inc., 1973.
Shor, Ira. Critical Teaching and Everyday Life.
   Chicago: University of Chicago Press, 1987.

For Students:

Anno, Mitsumasa. Anno's Math Games III.
   New York: Philomel Books, 1991.
Elffers, Joost. Tangram—The Ancient Chinese Shapes Game.
   New York: Viking Penguin, Inc., 1988.
Fixx, James F. Solve It!: A Perplexing Profusion of Puzzles.
   Garden City, NY: Doubleday & Co., Inc., 1978
Morgenstern, Steve. Metric Puzzles, Tricks & Games.
   New York: Sterling Co., 1978.
Mosler, Gerard. The Puzzle School.
   Toronto: Fitzhenry & Whiteside Ltd., 1977.
Nozaki, Akihiro. Anno's Hat Tricks.
   New York: Philomel Books, 1985.
Phillips, Louis. 263 Brain Busters—Just How Smart Are You, Anyway?
   New York: Viking Kestrel, Inc.,1985.
Shalit, Nathan. Science Magic Tricks.
   New York: Holt, Rinehart, and Winston Ltd., 1981.
White, Laurence B. Jr. and Broekel, Ray. Math-A-Magic: Number Tricks for Magicians.
   Niles, IL: Albert Whitman & Co., 1990.

page 32 — School Days.

Books stacked smallest to largest: social studies, science, reading, language, math.

page 34 — Go with the Flow.

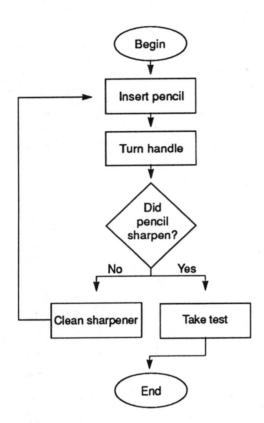

page 38 — Fishy Business.

1. 75 oz. (2.1 kg.)
2. 66 oz. (1.9 kg.)
3. 9 oz. (.3 kg.)
4. 6 oz. (.2 kg.)
5. The amount of water in each bag needs to be subtracted to determine the weight of the fish.

POWER PLAY: Largest to smallest: spotted, striped, plain.

page 39 — You Can Do It!

1. 9 cards in the bottom row of a stack of 45.
2. The placement of cans begins at the bottom row and builds upwards. (Answers may vary.)
3. One more can is added to each row. (Answers may vary.)
4. 24 cans in the last row of a stack of 300.